CHIHULY IN THE HOTSHOP

CHIHULY IN THE
HOTSHOP

CONTENTS

PREFACE

For thousands of years, the craft of glassmaking has remained a carefully guarded secret. By way of example, in 1291 the doges of Venice imposed an edict on the industry forcing its relocation to the island of Murano, to better monitor the industry and protect its secrets. Renegade workers who traveled beyond the republic to other glass centers were fined and imprisoned. Even today, it would be unthinkable for a master glassblower equipped with a camera to appear uninvited in another factory—much less accompanied by a film crew.

When the American studio glass movement took shape in the universities and craft schools of the early 1960s, things became more transparent, in part because the techniques of the craft were mostly unknown to the participants. Sharing information was vital if this community wanted to advance. That said, some artisans remain secretive to this day about how they make their work.

As a Fulbright scholar at the Venini glass factory on Murano in 1968, Dale Chihuly observed how the Venetians worked faster and produced more refined work as a team. In contrast, the American craftsmen at that time worked alone, adversely affecting the quality and achievable scale of their work. As a young professor at the

Rhode Island School of Design, Chihuly began to refine his notion of teamwork and to move toward an open-source approach.

Chihuly and his band of itinerant glassblowers, also known as gaffers, traveled together, giving workshops and making his work. He became a man with a mission, inspiring people to work with glass through events infused with energy. The team worked hard and played hard, at the end of the day feasting on Italian food and partying into the night. The pursuit of such camaraderie helped establish a sense of community. Chihuly has worked with hundreds of people over the years, some at the top of their game, others aspiring students. Some telephoned Chihuly out of the blue while others directed unsolicited letters proposing their candidacy. All the artists and gaffers who appear in this film are considered the best in the field today.

Chihuly acts on a hunch or gut feeling. He has this uncanny ability to spot talent or see things in people they may have not yet seen in themselves. He teaches by example, pushing people to work at the edge and go beyond their known capabilities. He tells them never to be afraid to fail. Part choreographer and part bandleader, Chihuly builds and modifies the teams on an as-needed basis to execute a never-ending series of ideas. He works in a zone that can only be referred to as controlled chaos.

The history of glass has been primarily concerned with the making of symmetrical forms. Chihuly noticed early on that glass doesn't necessarily tend to stay on center or want to conform to geometric forms. Often the gaffer needs to tease or even force the molten glass back on center. Chihuly quickly realized that this tendency in glass was something to exploit. He began to see the beauty in letting the molten glass go off center, making compelling organic shapes. Rather than rely on tools, he began to use heat, gravity, and centrifugal force, letting the inherent properties of glass help develop the shapes.

Chihuly had made one of the most important breakthroughs in the history of the medium. Armed with this new way of seeing, he set out to develop some of the most influential glass made in the twentieth century. Chihuly went about making thinner and more refined and technically complex shapes. He made groups or sets of objects while increasing the scale of the work. His ambitions soon took leave of the pedestal and became small installations on the floor. Chihuly kept pushing the scale, and soon the installations filled whole galleries. He has continued to make the work larger and taken it outdoors, where he installs it in formal gardens and directly out in nature.

In 2006, the Museum of Glass in Tacoma, Washington, invited Chihuly to work in its state-of-the-art hotshop, an amphitheater specifically designed to allow the audience to watch the action close at hand. Chihuly's residency soon became the idea for this documentary, as he set forth on an ambitious program that would reflect the sum total of his work in glass over the last thirty years, revisiting thirteen of his best-known series along with more than forty artists and gaffers who had worked with him at the time of the inception of each series.

Watch this electrifying performance as Chihuly runs through these series in the order in which they developed, and see how one thing leads to the other. Enjoy the wonderful Tom Tom Club soundtrack!

Mark McDonnell
Producer

ARTISTS and GAFFERS

Dale Chihuly

CYLINDERS Richard Royal
Joey Kirkpatrick and Flora C. Mace

BASKETS
William Morris with James Mongrain

SEAFORMS
Benjamin Moore

MACCHIA
William Morris with James Mongrain

SOFT CYLINDERS William Morris
Joey Kirkpatrick and Flora C. Mace

PERSIANS
Martin Blank

VENETIANS
Lino Tagliapietra

PICCOLO VENETIANS
Dante Marioni with Paul Cunningham

PUTTI Pino Signoretto
Amber Hauch and Paul DeSomma

IKEBANA
James Mongrain

NIIJIMA FLOATS
Richard Royal

PILCHUCK STUMPS
Martin Blank with Robbie Miller

FIORI
Joseph DeCamp

GET SET, GO

Between August 8 and 13, 2006, and again on February 3, 2007, Dale Chihuly was reunited at the Museum of Glass in Tacoma, Washington, with eleven of his original head glassblowers, or "gaffers," with whom he had created thirteen of his greatest earlier series. Seen by nearly 10,000 visitors in The Jane Russell Hot Shop at the Museum of Glass, the Tacoma blows were more than a reunion; they brought together artist and gaffers with enhanced and increased skill levels in order to reapproach and reinterpret the core of Chihuly's sculptural achievements.

Building on series of blown-glass objects that began as early as 1974 and as late as 2003, Chihuly renewed encounters with many of his signature ideas and merged these with the wealth of experience that came in between the first blows and the homecoming at the Museum of Glass. His hiring and cultivation of, and collaboration with, the eleven masters and a shifting resident team of thirty different glass-workers combined a long-standing precedent of technical expertise and excellence with the bravura visual excitement of the actual glassmaking processes reflected in filmmakers Peter West and Mark McDonnell's documentary footage on this DVD.

Seeing Chihuly as an artist of nonlinear development, that is, one who jumps ahead only to cross back, refine, and revisit earlier ideas that are altered, reconsidered, and refigured to new creative ends, the viewer will marvel at the artist's ceaseless invention and imagination.

Aided by the initial gaffers of each stylistic grouping, and the virtually telepathic support system of the often-overlapping team members, Chihuly's constant changes and improvements are executed before our eyes. How and why each series was invented and reconceived at the Museum of Glass is examined below.

CYLINDERS

Navajo Blanket Cylinder, 1984, 12 x 7 x 7"

The *Black Cylinders* (2006–) are a variant on Chihuly's first series, the *Cylinders* (1974–). Evolved by Chihuly and early Pilchuck Glass School collaborators Italo Scanga and James Carpenter as a way to do drawing on glass, they are characterized by delicate, thinly sliced pieces of glass that create patterns or "pick-up" drawings (the glass picks up the thin shards and threads when rolled over them while still hot). This kind of surface decoration was an important technical breakthrough for American studio glass in general and for Chihuly in particular. Never before had such exact drawings and images been applied to hot glass in quite this way.

First executed with the slicing, cutting, and arranging into patterns done according to Chihuly's wishes by Kate Elliott, whom Chihuly met at Pilchuck Glass School in 1974, the *Cylinders* were developed at Pilchuck Glass School and the Rhode Island School of Design with the assistance of two other women glassblowers, Joey Kirkpatrick (who set out the designs on the heated steel table, or marver) and Flora C. Mace (who made the "pick-up" drawings).

Black Cylinder #26
2006, 20 x 8 x 8"

BASKETS

Begun in earnest in 1977, the *Baskets* were inspired by Chihuly's seeing a visible-storage display of the Coast Salish tribe's woven cedar-bark baskets at the Washington State Historical Society in Tacoma. In order to approximate the casual look of the Northwest Coast Native American models stacked within one another and sagging from their own weight, Chihuly jettisoned a long Italian glassblowing tradition, symmetry, and deliberately attempted an asymmetrical, off-kilter look to each vessel. Further emulating the look of the Indian baskets in storage, Chihuly invented a new way of positioning glass—the stacked set.

Although Benjamin Moore began the series as gaffer, William Morris and the Tacoma blow team concentrated on enlarging and perfecting the defining aspects of the original *Baskets*: an incomparably thin wall; backgrounds of muted colors; an extension of the "pick-up" drawings from the *Cylinders*; and more innovative solutions to the nested and stacked compositions.

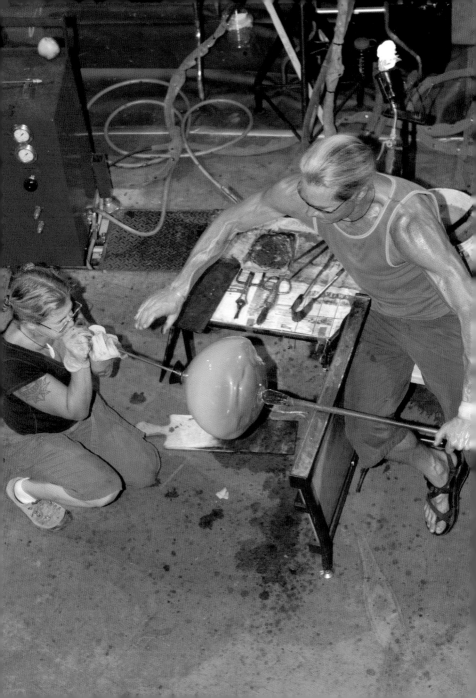

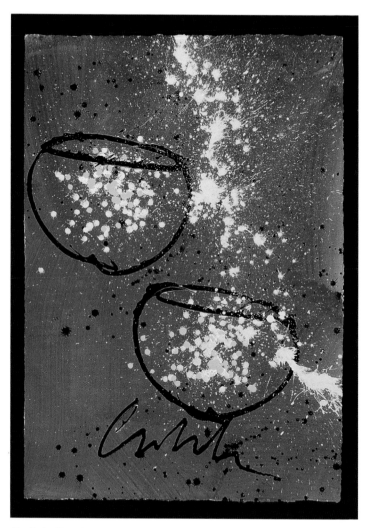

Baskets Drawing
2005, 42 x 30"

SEAFORMS

The *Seaforms* (1980–) proceed from Chihuly's motto, "Follow nature." Building on his childhood memories of beachcombing along Puget Sound, the *Seaforms* attain even thinner glass walls than the *Baskets*, thanks partly to the use of a ribbed optical mold into which the glass is blown.

Corinthian Pink and White Seaform Set with Jet Lip Wraps
2002, 11 x 21 x 15"

With their translucent walls, horizontal patterning due to the mold, and pale, ethereal colors, the *Seaforms* brought Chihuly much of his early national and international acclaim. Compared to jellyfish, oyster shells, and other mollusks, the *Seaforms* are the first of the artist's series to convey ecological content, reminding us of the fragility of the marine environment. More symmetrical than the *Baskets* and even-sided, the *Seaforms*, when stacked or piled in sets, resemble coral reefs or underwater colonies of invertebrate organisms.

At the time of the original *Seaforms*, Benjamin Moore and William Morris each worked as lead gaffer. Gradually over a period of time, thanks to the increased skills of Moore, who returned to Tacoma, and to larger studio equipment not available before, the size of the *Seaforms*, as well as their scale and the number in each set, increased as well. In the Tacoma blow, ever-thinner walls with sophisticated, delicate colors contribute to the overall impression that the *Seaforms* are Chihuly's first fully created imaginary world. They led to one of his first permanent installations, *Puget Sound Forms* (1987) at the Seattle Aquarium.

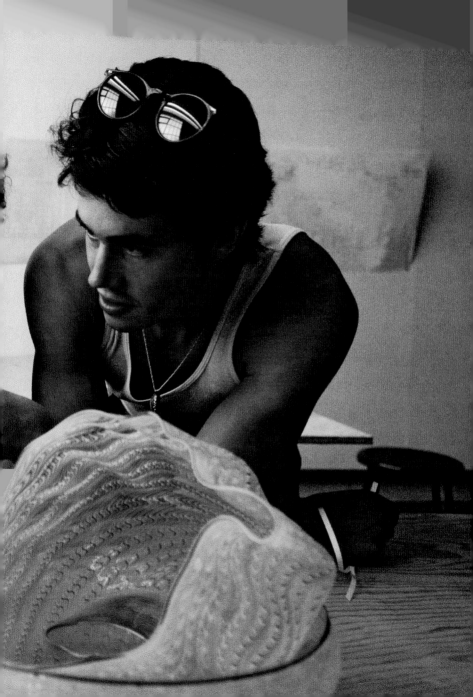

Following pages
*White Seaform Set
with White Lip Wraps*
1987, 5 x 18 x 12"

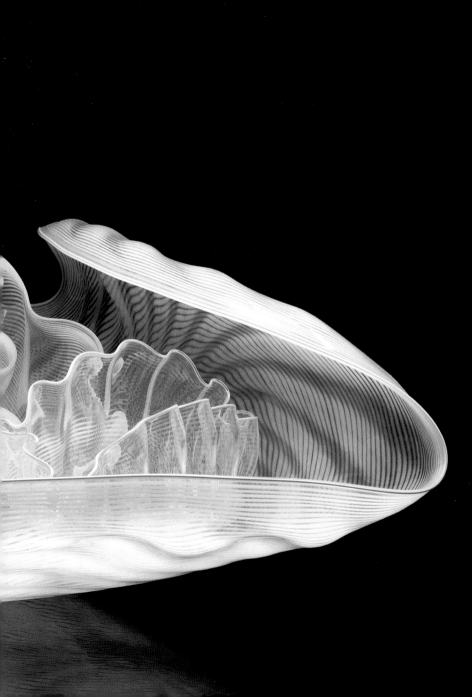

MACCHIA

*Armenian Blue
Macchia with Burnt
Sienna Lip Wrap
1981, 4 x 8 x 7"*

Starting in 1981, the *Macchia* arose out of an interesting challenge: Chihuly wanted to try to use all 300 colors available in the pre-manufactured Kugler glass rods that are the building blocks of blown glass. *Macchia* has many definitions in Italian, but for Chihuly's purpose it means spots or speckles, and was suggested by his close friend the Italian-American artist Italo Scanga. With both the inner and outer surfaces of each vessel employed for placement of the spots, the carefully selected colors complement one another and sometimes clash when viewed through the translucent walls. The sliced bits of glass that become the spots and speckles are laid out on a steel table called a marver, and then are rolled over by the hot glass on the end of the blowpipe. These are called "jimmies." The jimmies become the chromatic elements of each *macula*, the original Latin word for spot.

When William Morris, the original gaffer on the series along with Benjamin Moore, worked at the Museum of Glass on August 13, 2006, artist and gaffer were assisted by a team, all under the supervision of Chihuly. Taking the opportunity to revisit one of his most spectacular yet technically complicated series, Chihuly asked the blowers and their helpers to make *Macchia* of increasingly greater sizes, up to thirty inches in diameter.

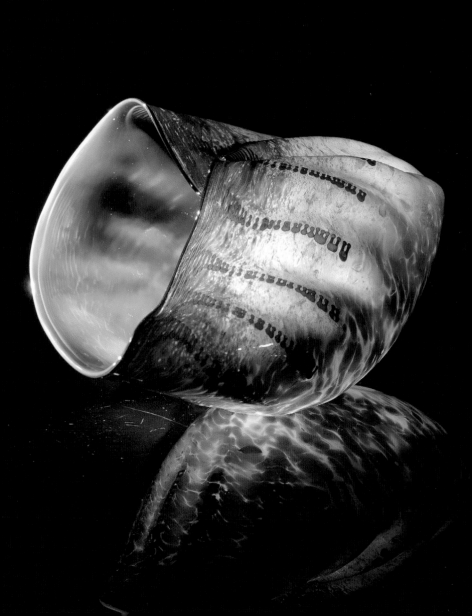

Russet Orange Macchia
with Lime Lip Wrap
2006, 22 x 38 x 32"

SOFT CYLINDERS

*Turquoise Green
Soft Cylinder with
Ochre Drawing
1988, 17 x 17 x 14"*

Three of Chihuly's most important early team members, William Morris, Flora C. Mace, and Joey Kirkpatrick, joined him on August 13, 2006, to re-create the *Soft Cylinders* (1986–). Building on the original, straight-sided *Cylinders* (1974), the *Soft Cylinders* combine aspects of the artist's first significant series with innovations such as inflated size and asymmetrical, collapsed shapes.

Much of Chihuly's achievement has involved stretching the strict limits of classical Venetian glassblowing; the *Soft Cylinders* are good examples of this outward extension. Their upright walls (as opposed to graceful curves) as well as their use of the "pick-up" drawings (as opposed to enameling applied and fired later) are different from traditional Italian models, as are their increased size and irregular profiles that reflect the pull of gravity on the great weight of glass while on the blowpipe.

PERSIANS

The rage for antique Persian glass, due to late-nineteenth-century archaeological digs throughout the Middle East and Mediterranean Basin, has been cleverly exploited nearly a century later in Chihuly's *Persians* (1986–), which were reconceived with Martin Blank, their original gaffer, in Tacoma on August 9, 2006.

Jaffa Orange Persian Set with Graphite Lip Wraps, 2000, 11 x 18 x 14"

Chihuly answered Louis Comfort Tiffany's celebrated Favrile glass, which also emulated Persian glass artifacts through Tiffany's patented oxidizing process, making the surfaces look iridescent and aged, as if just excavated. Without trying to reproduce Tiffany's antique look, Chihuly's *Persians* do share narrow necks and fluted or flared lips, as if they were ancient teardrop containers or perfume flasks, as well as generally darker wall colors.

The *Persians* are Chihuly's first series to consciously suggest historical revivalism. They were also the subject of the artist's first critical controversy: a spat between two New York art critics, Roberta Smith of the *New York Times* and Rose Slivka of the *East Hampton Star*, when the *Persians* debuted at the Dia Art Foundation in Bridgehampton, New York, in 1988. Discussing the Persians, Slivka asked pointedly, "How beautiful can it be and still be art? Can a thing be too beautiful?" The enthusiastic response of viewers and other curators long ago decided the answer to that question.

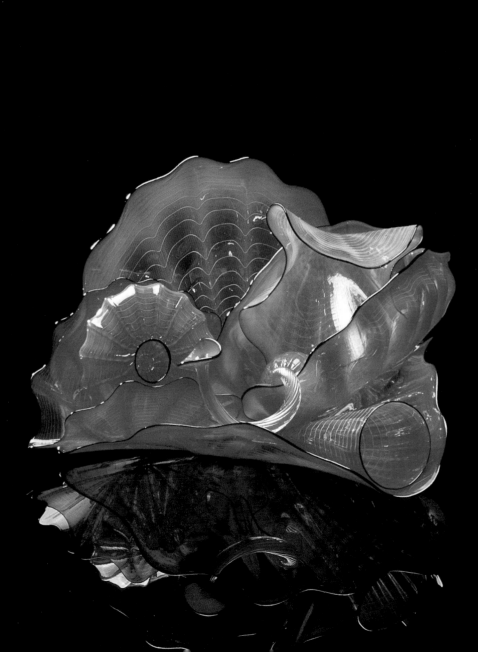

VENETIANS

Black Venetian with Lapis Leaves
2006, 28 x 12 x 16"

Among the most analyzed of Chihuly's series, the *Venetians* (1988–) were revisited on February 3, 2007, by their original master, Lino Tagliapietra, considered by many (including Chihuly) to be the greatest glassblower in the world. With their opulent colors, extravagant size, and showy technical effects (like the elaborate glass roping that wraps around some of them), the *Venetians* are more fantasies about early- to mid-twentieth-century Italian glass than strict historical tributes.

Inspired by seeing a private collection of Italian glass art of the 1923–45 period in a family palazzo in Venice, Chihuly began the *Venetians* with Tagliapietra in Seattle in 1988 and continued the series with Richard Royal and others joining Tagliapietra or working on their own under Chihuly in 1989, 1990, and 1991. Tagliapietra has continued working on them periodically to the present.

Drawing upon the faint resemblance to machine-like forms and geometric structures of Italian Art Deco glass artists such as Napoleone Martinuzzi, Ercole Barovier, and Vittorio Zecchin, the *Venetians* go beyond the Italian masters, into Chihuly's second fully created world of historical revivalism after the *Persians*.

With the insertion of spiky handles, gold and silver metallic leaf, bubbly walls, and color combinations only Chihuly could have conceived of, the *Venetians* of the Tacoma blow add a culminating chapter to the series. Thanks to Tagliapietra's unprecedented skills, the graceful yet tight qualities of the historical models are now matched under Chihuly's direction by an American as well as Italian swagger.

Saturn Red Piccolo Venetian
with Pale Gold Ridged Prunts
2002, 10 x 13 x 13"

PICCOLO VENETIANS

*Red Piccolo Venetian
with Blue Lip
Wrap and Handles
1998, 13 x 11 x 11"*

The *Piccolo Venetians* (1993–) are a refinement of the *Venetians* (1988–). First executed for Chihuly by Lino Tagliapietra, the *Piccolo Venetians* are an attempt to devise a more intimate object, one with a reduced size that better allows for intricately coiling wraps and other additions, known collectively as "bit work." In Tacoma, Dante Marioni and Paul Cunningham (who had worked with Tagliapietra on the first *Piccolos*) returned on August 11, 2006, to supplement the series, some of which are displayed in small groupings or sets.

With thinner walls closer to the Italian originals, the *Piccolo Venetians* also have more delicate colors—pale chartreuse, pink, and orange—with simple black accents. The glass of the *Piccolos* has a clear quality, while many of the first *Venetians* have thicker, darker, and more bubbly sides.

Just as Chihuly drew upon Tagliapietra's skills to create bigger, more spectacular works appropriate to his tribute to the pre–World War II Venetian designers, so he challenged Marioni, an American who first visited Murano at the age of sixteen, to complement Tagliapietra's achievements without the hefty bulk. Tightly focused, elegant, and graceful, the *Piccolo Venetians* are lighthearted caprices, instantly endearing and appealing.

Yellow Gold Piccolo
Venetian with Handles
1998, 10 x 10 x 11"

PUTTI

*Gilded Mystic Blue
Putti Venetian with
Swan and Cherubs
1994, 19 x 15 x 15"*

One result of the *Venetians* was the search for additions that could retain the elegant shapes of the vessels while reflecting yet more examples of bravura technical skills associated with Europe. Chihuly found the answer in Giuseppe "Pino" Signoretto, perhaps the greatest of the Italian masters of *massiccio*, or solid-glass sculpture.

Begun in 1989 while Signoretto was a visiting artist at Pilchuck Glass School, the *Putti* added small cherubs, baby angels, and cupid figures (said by some to be portraits of Chihuly) to the *Venetians*, becoming their own distinct series. Over the next few years, the figures overlapped with other series, appearing on *Ikebana*, *Pilchuck Stumps*, and *Chandeliers*. They represent Chihuly's first sculptural use of the human figure.

Perched on the rims of oversize vessels, the figures introduced narrative elements into each piece. With Signoretto working in Tacoma on August 12, 2006, assisted by Amber Hauch and Paul DeSomma, the new *Putti* continued Chihuly's original idea of adding figures to create stories. They joined other works in which the *Putti* had been appended to sea creatures, dolphins, starfish, and clamshells, all in the artist's attempt to develop a style of glass that would be enjoyed especially by children, as well as adults.

*Black Sea Anemone
and Fish on Gilt
Striped Vessel*
2006, 36 x 21 x 21"

IKEBANA

Fire Coral Ikebana
with Cascading Stem
1993, 29 x 47 x 16"

When Chihuly was approached in Japan by a master of ikebana, the Japanese art of flower arranging, to use one of his vases to make an arrangement with real flowers, he thought, "Why not make the flowers, too?" and the *Ikebana* (1990–) were born. It followed naturally upon the artist's longtime interest in flowers and also developed from an earlier installation piece, *Flower Forms #2* (1986), at the Sheraton Seattle Hotel and Towers.

Begun with Lino Tagliapietra, the *Ikebana* were further developed by James Mongrain. Chihuly was joined at the Museum of Glass on February 3, 2007, by Mongrain and other veteran team members. Together they fabricated new variants on the wildly linear stems, the erratic twining of the leaf, and the open form of the blossoms set into bulging single-, double-, and triple-form vases beneath. The fecundity of nature is reflected in the pregnant, stacked-gourd forms (alluding to Chinese and Islamic ceramics) and the bursting forth of the blooms.

With the reassembled team of artist, gaffer, and crew, the *Ikebana* of the Tacoma blow underscored the simplicity of single- or double-stem flowers in real Japanese arrangements—but brought them to the more explosive and colorful level associated with Chihuly's art.

Following pages
*Ruby Dappled Chartreuse Ikebana with Fiery
Red Stems,* Garfield Park Conservatory,
Chicago, Illinois, 2001

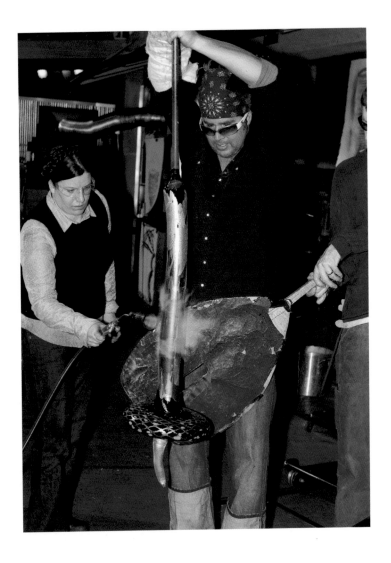

Buddha Red Ikebana with Yellow and Scarlet Stems
Fairchild Tropical Botanic Garden, Coral Gables,
Florida, 2006, 55 x 45 x 20"

NIIJIMA FLOATS

Chihuly a Spoleto,
Spoleto, Italy, 1995,
20 x 20 x 20'

First seen in an important installation at the American Craft Museum (now the Museum of Arts & Design, New York) in 1992, the *Niijima Floats* (1991–) also grew out of a trip to Japan. Visiting the small glassblowing center on Niijima Island in Tokyo Bay, Chihuly found a reciprocal opportunity: he could make giant glass fishing floats like the smaller ones he had found washed up on the beaches of Puget Sound as a child. Quickly, they became the largest objects ever blown in glass, as well as the heaviest.

Thanks to the Herculean efforts of master gaffer Richard Royal (who rejoined Chihuly and the team on August 10, 2006), the *Niijima Floats* are not only echoes of smaller fishing-net floats; they are symbols of the world globe covered and "mapped" by the applications of hundreds of "jimmies" and silver and gold leaf.

Like the *Ikebana*, the *Niijima Floats* pay tribute to Japanese culture and to historical ties between the Pacific Northwest and Japan. Transmuted through the dazzling glories of Italian glassblowing skills transferred to the United States by Chihuly, the *Niijima Floats* operate as cross-cultural ambassadors endorsing the simplicity of Japanese maritime craft traditions and the eye-popping, over-the-top artistic demonstrations of Chihuly's own global vision.

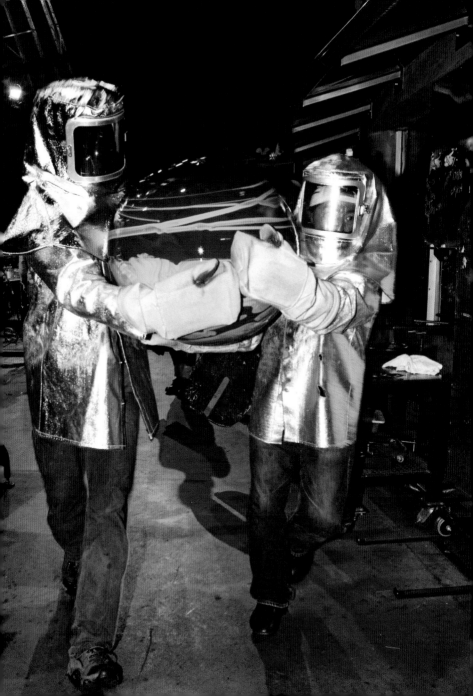

PILCHUCK STUMPS

*Lime Yellow Pilchuck
Stump with Gold Leaf*
1992, 23 x 10 x 10"

Since Pilchuck Glass School is surrounded by a wilderness of trees, Chihuly's *Pilchuck Stumps* (1992–) make perfect sense. Beginning as elements for Chihuly's 1992 Seattle Art Museum installation exhibition, and continuing as scenic elements for a 1993 Seattle Opera production of Debussy's 1906 opera, *Pelléas et Mélisande, Pilchuck Stumps* were developed in tandem with columned Mylar versions for the stage.

With their bizarre iridescent sheen, which echoes Tiffany's Favrile glass, the *Pilchuck Stumps* were initially blown by gaffer Martin Blank and were re-created by Blank and Robbie Miller under Chihuly's guidance at the Museum of Glass on August 11, 2006.

Blown into specially built wooden molds that form the exterior "bark" of each piece, the works in the Tacoma blow increased in size, in some cases approaching four feet long. Chihuly employed a titanium-oxide spray, applied to the glass once it was removed from the molds; that approximated Tiffany's iridizing process, but with a greater range of color tones, from deep blue and green to dark orange, brown, and black.

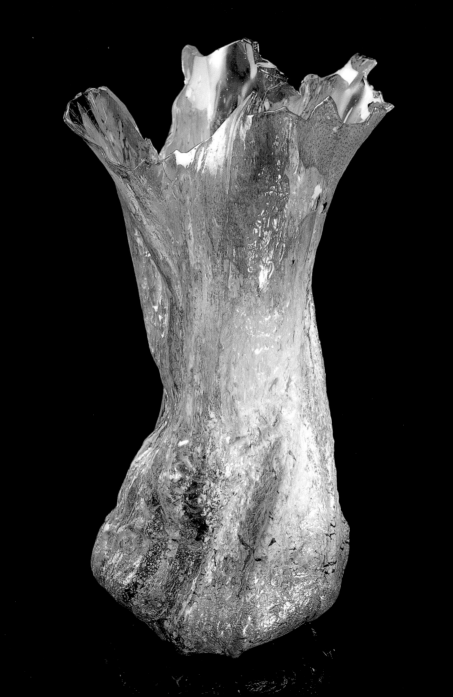

Both alive- and dead-looking, *Pilchuck Stumps* reinforce ecology as an underlying theme in all of Chihuly's art. They symbolize the entire cycle of modern forests: growth, death, reseeding, harvesting, planting, and renewal— the same cycle over and over, just as Chihuly has reinterpreted his own various series.

Transparent Compose Green Pilchuck Stump
1992, 11 x 32 x 12"

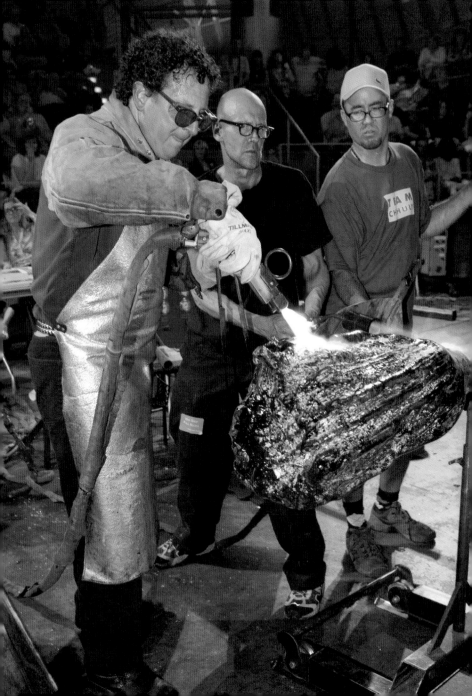

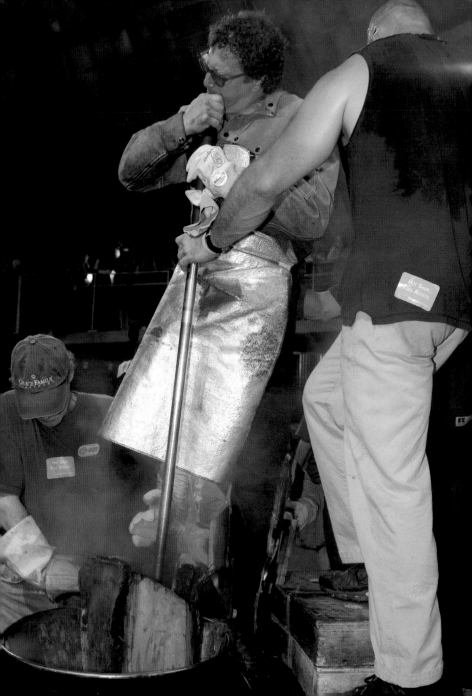

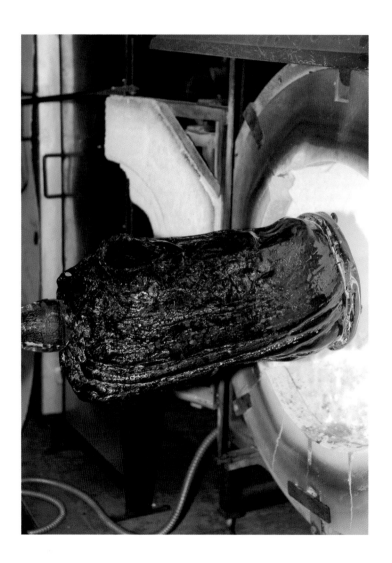

FIORI

Paintbrushes
Medina, Washington,
2006

The *Fiori* (2003–) are the outgrowth of three prior series: the *Ikebana* (Chihuly's first serious floral motif); the works done in Nuutajärvi, Finland, in 1996 in preparation for the artist's series of indoor and outdoor installations in Venice later that year; and *Mille Fiore*, one of Chihuly's largest temporary installations, displayed at the Tacoma Art Museum in 2003.

Bigger, bolder, and more diverse than their inspirations and forerunners, the *Fiori* are also a pun on a Venetian glass standby, *mille fiore*: long glass ropes of tightly packed, contrastingly colored glass rods that are then cut up, salami-style, and said to resemble "a thousand flowers."

Joseph DeCamp made the first *Fiori* in Seattle at Chihuly's request. The *Fiori* comprise the widest vocabulary of different shapes in any Chihuly series thus far. Long stems, generalized blossoms, saguaro cactus shapes, water lilies, and other botanical elements, such as leaves, seeds, and buds, come together in installations Chihuly has designed for public conservatories in the United States and, significantly, at the Royal Botanic Gardens, Kew, near London. They are also displayed in smaller groupings set on pedestals.

Technically, DeCamp made exaggerated spears, clumps, twists, twirls, and leaf ends for the *Fiori* in Tacoma, some as long as twelve feet. They confirm Chihuly's celebration and glorification of nature, reminding us that flowers and gardens, like glass art, are cultivated, human constructions subject to the same elements as the natural environment: heat, light, water, and air.

Mille Fiori
Tacoma, Washington,
2003

CLOSING As the edited documentary film accompanying these comments demonstrates, the art of Dale Chihuly is one of retraced pathways, revisited locales, and fully imagined worlds occupied by his blown-glass sculptures. The excitement of the blow sessions is captured vividly, complete with suspenseful, perilous moments when all seems close to collapse, loss, or triumph. The individual series each have a history based on Chihuly's personal experiences; his knowledge of art history and the decorative-arts traditions of the United States, Italy, Japan, and elsewhere; and his grasp of how to make the teams fulfill his wishes. Set in the context of the above descriptions, briefly chronicling the series' origins and developments, this may help viewers gain an understanding of Chihuly's evolution as an artist and his circuitous methods of creation, inspiration, and refinement, as well as see how individual works make the journey from drawing to blowpipe to annealing oven and, finally, to the museum or gallery where they begin their existence out in the world.

Matthew Kangas

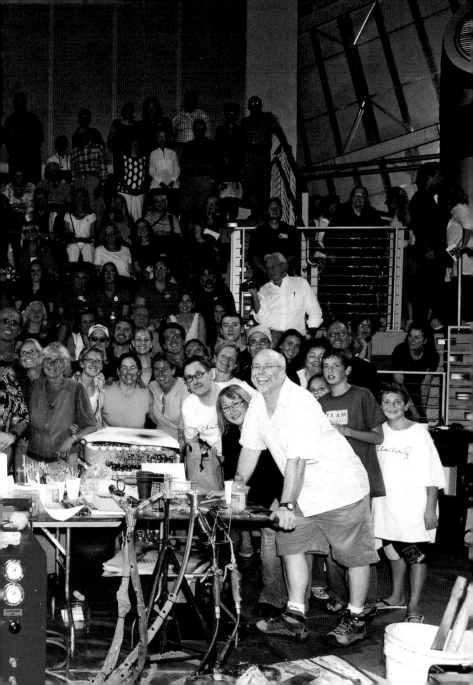

CREDITS

We would like to thank everyone who participated in the making of this film.

Dale Chihuly

Leslie Jackson Chihuly

Billy O'Neill, Executive Producer

Jenny Brown
Ken Clark
Barbara DuBois
Heather Gray
Leanne Hart
Michael Hytinen
Scott Mitchell Leen
Janet Makela
Teresa Nouri Rishel
Terry Rishel
Barry Rosen
Joanna Sikes
Charlie Wilkins
Kim Williams
Everyone at the Chihuly Studio
Seattle, Washington

Timothy Close, Director / CEO
Museum of Glass Board of Trustees
Liz Cepanec
Julie Pisto
Todd Pottinger
Susan Warner
The entire staff at the Museum of Glass
Tacoma, Washington

Chris Frantz and Tina Weymouth
Jennifer, Finn and Ariel

CHIHULY IN THE HOTSHOP

PRODUCED BY
Mark McDonnell

DIRECTED BY
Peter West

EDITED BY
Peter West
John Campbell

CINEMATOGRAPHY
Joseph Hudson
Bruce Hutson
Peter West

SOUND RECORDING
Matt Monroe
Eric Reeves

RE–RECORDING MIXER
Matt Gruber

PRODUCTION ASSISTANTS
Isabelle McDonnell
Damien Villarreal

INTERVIEWS BY
Mark McDonnell
Peter West

MUSIC
Tom Tom Club

CHRONOLOGY

1941 Born September 20 in Tacoma, Washington, to George Chihuly and Viola Magnuson Chihuly.

1957 Older brother and only sibling, George, is killed in a Naval Air Force training accident in Pensacola, Florida.

1958 His father suffers a fatal heart attack at age 51. His mother goes to work to support herself and Dale.

1959 Graduates from high school in Tacoma. Enrolls in the College of Puget Sound (now the University of Puget Sound) in his hometown. Transfers to the University of Washington in Seattle to study interior design and architecture.

1961 Joins Delta Kappa Epsilon fraternity and becomes rush chairman. Learns to melt and fuse glass.

1962 Disillusioned with his studies, he leaves school and travels to Florence to study art. Discouraged by not being able to speak Italian, he leaves and travels to the Middle East.

1963 Works on a kibbutz in the Negev Desert. Returns to the University of Washington in the College of Arts and Sciences and studies under Hope Foote and Warren Hill. In a weaving class with Doris Brockway, he incorporates glass shards into woven tapestries.

1964 Returns to Europe, visits Leningrad, and makes the first of many trips to Ireland.

1965 Receives B.A. in Interior Design from the University of Washington. Experimenting on his own in his basement studio, Chihuly blows his first glass bubble by melting stained glass and using a metal pipe.

1966 Works as a commercial fisherman in Alaska to earn money for graduate school. Enters the University of Wisconsin at Madison, where he studies glassblowing under Harvey Littleton.

1967 Receives M.S. in Sculpture from the University of Wisconsin. Enrolls at the Rhode Island School of Design (RISD) in Providence, where he begins his exploration of environmental works using neon, argon, and blown glass. Awarded a Louis Comfort Tiffany Foundation Grant for work in glass. Italo Scanga, then on the faculty at Pennsylvania State University's Art Department, lectures at RISD, and the two begin a lifelong friendship.

1968 Receives M.F.A. in Ceramics from RISD. Awarded a Fulbright Fellowship, which enables him to travel and work in Europe. Becomes the first American glassblower to work in the Venini factory on the island of Murano. Returns to the United States and spends four consecutive summers teaching at Haystack Mountain School of Crafts in Deer Isle, Maine.

1969 Travels again throughout Europe and meets glass masters Erwin Eisch in Germany and Jaroslava Brychtová and Stanislav Libenský in Czechoslovakia. Returning to the United States, Chihuly establishes the glass program at RISD, where he teaches for the next fifteen years.

1970 Meets James Carpenter, a student in the RISD Illustration Department, and they begin a four-year collaboration.

1971 On the site of a tree farm donated by Seattle art patrons Anne Gould Hauberg and John Hauberg, the Pilchuck Glass School is founded. Chihuly's first environmental installation at Pilchuck is created that summer. He resumes teaching at RISD and creates *20,000 Pounds of Ice and Neon*, *Glass Forest #1*, and *Glass Forest #2* with James Carpenter, installations that prefigure later environmental works by Chihuly.

1972 Continues to collaborate with Carpenter on large-scale architectural projects. They create *Rondel Door* and *Cast Glass Door* at Pilchuck. Back in Providence, they create *Dry Ice, Bent Glass and Neon*, a conceptual breakthrough.

1974 Supported by a National Endowment for the Arts grant at Pilchuck, James Carpenter, a group of students, and he develop a technique for picking up glass thread drawings. In December at RISD, he completes his last collaborative project with Carpenter, *Corning Wall*.

1975 At RISD, begins series of *Navajo Blanket Cylinders*. Kate Elliott and, later, Flora C. Mace fabricate the complex thread drawings. He receives the first of two National Endowment for the Arts Individual Artist grants. Artist-in-residence with Seaver Leslie at Artpark, on the Niagara Gorge, in New York State. Begins *Irish Cylinders* and *Ulysses Cylinders* with Leslie and Mace.

1976 An automobile accident in England leaves him, after weeks in the hospital and 256 stitches in his face, without sight in his left eye and with permanent damage to his right ankle and foot. After recuperating he returns to Providence to serve as head of the Department of Sculpture and the Program in Glass at RISD. Henry Geldzahler, curator of contemporary art at the Metropolitan Museum of Art in New York, acquires three *Navajo Blanket Cylinders* for the museum's collection. This is a turning point in Chihuly's career, and a friendship between artist and curator commences.

1977 Inspired by Northwest Coast Indian baskets he sees at the Washington State Historical Society in Tacoma, begins the *Basket* series at Pilchuck over the summer, with Benjamin Moore as his assistant gaffer. Continues his bicoastal teaching assignments, dividing his time between Rhode Island and the Pacific Northwest.

1978 Meets William Morris, a student at Pilchuck Glass School, and the two begin a close, eight-year working relationship. A solo show, *Baskets and Cylinders*, curated by Michael W. Monroe at the Renwick Gallery, Smithsonian Institution, in Washington, D.C., is another career milestone.

1979 Dislocates his shoulder in a bodysurfing accident and relinquishes the gaffer position for good. William Morris becomes his chief gaffer for the next several years. Chihuly begins to make drawings as a way to communicate his designs.

1980 Resigns his teaching position at RISD. He returns there periodically during the 1980s as artist-in-residence. Begins *Seaform* series at Pilchuck in the summer and later, back in Providence, returns to architectural installations with the creation of windows for the Shaare Emeth Synagogue in St. Louis, Missouri.

1981 Begins *Macchia* series.

1982 First major catalog is published: *Chihuly Glass*, designed by RISD colleague and friend Malcolm Grear.

1983 Returns to the Pacific Northwest after sixteen years on the East Coast. Works at Pilchuck in the fall and winter, further developing the *Macchia* series with William Morris as chief gaffer.

1984 Begins work on the *Soft Cylinder* series, with Flora C. Mace and Joey Kirkpatrick executing the glass drawings.

1985 Begins working hot glass on a larger scale and creates several site-specific installations.

1986 Begins *Persian* series with Martin Blank as gaffer, assisted by Robbie Miller. With the opening of *Dale Chihuly objets de verre* at the Musée des Arts Décoratifs, Palais du Louvre, in Paris, he becomes one of only four American artists to have had a one-person exhibition at the Louvre.

1987 Establishes his first hotshop in the Van de Kamp Building near Lake Union. Begins association with artist Parks Anderson. Marries playwright Sylvia Peto.

1988 Inspired by a private collection of Italian Art Deco glass, Chihuly begins *Venetian* series. Working from Chihuly's drawings, Lino Tagliapietra serves as gaffer.

1989 With Italian glass masters Lino Tagliapietra, Pino Signoretto, and a team of glassblowers at Pilchuck Glass School, begins *Putti* series. Working with Tagliapietra, Chihuly creates *Ikebana* series, inspired by his travels to Japan and exposure to ikebana masters.

1990 Purchases the historic Pocock Building located on Lake Union, realizing his dream of being on the water in Seattle. Renovates the building and names it The Boathouse, for use as a studio, hotshop, and archives. Travels to Japan.

1991 Begins *Niijima Float* series with Richard Royal as gaffer, creating some of the largest pieces of glass ever blown by hand. Completes a number of architectural installations. He and Sylvia Peto divorce.

1992 Begins *Chandelier* series with a hanging sculpture at the Seattle Art Museum. Designs sets for Seattle Opera production of Debussy's *Pelléas et Mélisande*.

1993 Begins *Piccolo Venetian* series with Lino Tagliapietra. Creates *100,000 Pounds of Ice and Neon*, a temporary installation in the Tacoma Dome, Tacoma, Washington.

1994 Creates five installations for Tacoma's Union Station Federal Courthouse. Hilltop Artists-in-Residence, a glassblowing program for at-risk youths in Tacoma, Washington, is created by friend Kathy Kaperick. Within two years the program partners with Tacoma Public Schools, and Chihuly remains a strong role model and adviser.

1995 *Chihuly Over Venice* begins with a glassblowing session in Nuutajärvi, Finland, and a subsequent blow at the Waterford Crystal factory, Ireland.

1996 *Chihuly Over Venice* continues with a blow in Monterrey, Mexico, and culminates with the installation of fourteen *Chandeliers* at various sites in Venice. Creates his first permanent outdoor installation, *Icicle Creek Chandelier*.

1997 Continues and expands series of experimental plastics he calls Polyvitro. *Chihuly* is designed by Massimo Vignelli and copublished by Harry N. Abrams, Inc., New York, and Portland Press, Seattle. A permanent installation of Chihuly's work opens at the Hakone Glass Forest, Ukai Museum, in Hakone, Japan.

1998 Chihuly is invited to Sydney, Australia, with his team to participate in the Sydney Arts Festival. A son, Jackson Viola Chihuly, is born February 12 to Dale Chihuly and Leslie Jackson. Creates architectural installations for Benaroya Hall, Seattle; Bellagio, Las Vegas; and Atlantis, the Bahamas.

1999 Begins *Jerusalem Cylinder* series with gaffer James Mongrain, in concert with Flora C. Mace and Joey Kirkpatrick. Mounts his most ambitious exhibition to date: *Chihuly in the Light of Jerusalem 2000*, at the Tower of David Museum of the History of Jerusalem. Outside the museum he creates a sixty-foot wall from twenty-four massive blocks of ice shipped from Alaska.

2000 Creates *La Tour de Lumière* sculpture as part of the exhibition *Contemporary American Sculpture* in Monte Carlo. Marlborough Gallery represents Chihuly. More than a million visitors enter the Tower of David Museum to see *Chihuly in the Light of Jerusalem 2000*, breaking the world attendance record for a temporary exhibition during 1999–2000.

2001 The Victoria and Albert Museum, in London, curates the exhibition *Chihuly at the V&A*. Exhibits at Marlborough Gallery, New York and London. Groups a series of *Chandeliers* for the first time to create an installation for the Mayo Clinic in Rochester, Minnesota. Artist Italo Scanga dies, friend and mentor for over three decades. Presents his first major glasshouse exhibition, *Chihuly in the Park: A Garden of Glass*, at the Garfield Park Conservatory, Chicago.

2002 Creates installations for the Salt Lake 2002 Olympic Winter Games. The Chihuly Bridge of Glass, conceived by Chihuly and designed in collaboration with Arthur Andersson of Andersson·Wise Architects, is dedicated in Tacoma, Washington.

2003 Begins the *Fiori* series for the opening exhibition at the Tacoma Art Museum's new building. TAM designs a permanent installation for its collection of his works. *Chihuly at the Conservatory* opens at the Franklin Park Conservatory, Columbus, Ohio.

2004 Creates new forms in his *Fiori* series for an exhibition at Marlborough Gallery, New York. The Orlando Museum of Art and the Museum of Fine Arts, St. Petersburg, Florida, become the first museums to collaborate and present simultaneous major exhibitions of his work. Presents a glasshouse exhibition at Atlanta Botanical Garden. Another collaborative exhibition opens in Los Angeles at the Frederick R. Weisman Museum of Art, L.A. Louver Gallery, and Frank Lloyd Gallery.

2005 Marries Leslie Jackson. Mounts a major garden exhibition at the Royal Botanic Gardens, Kew, outside London. Shows at Marlborough Monaco and Marlborough London. Exhibits at the Fairchild Tropical Botanic Garden, Coral Gables, Florida.

2006 Mother, Viola, dies at the age of ninety-eight in Tacoma, Washington. Presents glasshouse exhibits at the Missouri Botanical Garden and the New York Botanical Garden. *Chihuly in Tacoma*, hotshop sessions at the Museum of Glass, reunites Chihuly and glassblowers from important periods in his development.

2007 Exhibits at the Phipps Conservatory and Botanical Gardens, Pittsburgh.

COLOPHON

This first packaging of
CHIHULY IN THE HOTSHOP DVD and book
is limited to 7,500 casebound copies.
The entire contents are copyright © 2007
Dale Chihuly unless otherwise stated.
All rights reserved.

PHOTOGRAPHY

Shaun Chappell, Dale Chihuly, John Gaines,
Ira Garber, Claire Garoutte, Russell Johnson,
Scott Mitchell Leen, Teresa Nouri Rishel,
Terry Rishel, Roger Schreiber, Chuck Taylor,
and Ray Charles White

DESIGN

Anna Katherine Curfman and Briana Hesse

TYPEFACE

Franklin Gothic

PAPER

Lumisilk matt art 150 gsm

PRINTED AND BOUND BY

Global PSD in China

𝕋

Portland Press
PO Box 70856, Seattle, Washington 98127
800 574 7272 · www.portlandpress.net

ISBN 13: 978-1-57684-107-5
ISBN 10: 1-57684-107-3